SECOND EDITION

TOUCHSTONE

WORKBOOK 2A

MICHAEL MCCARTHY
JEANNE MCCARTEN
HELEN SANDIFORD

CAMBRIDGE
UNIVERSITY PRESS

Shaftesbury Road, Cambridge CB2 8EA, United Kingdom

One Liberty Plaza, 20th Floor, New York, NY 10006, USA

477 Williamstown Road, Port Melbourne, VIC 3207, Australia

314–321, 3rd Floor, Plot 3, Splendor Forum, Jasola District Centre, New Delhi – 110025, India

103 Penang Road, #05-06/07, Visioncrest Commercial, Singapore 238467

Cambridge University Press & Assessment is a department of the University of Cambridge.

We share the University's mission to contribute to society through the pursuit of education, learning and research at the highest international levels of excellence.

www.cambridge.org
Information on this title: www.cambridge.org/9781107649880

First published 2005
Second Edition 2014

20 19 18 17 16 15 14 13 12 11

Printed in Great Britain by Ashford Colour Press Ltd.

A catalog record for this publication is available from the British Library.

ISBN 978-1-107-68173-6 Student's Book
ISBN 978-1-107-68175-0 Student's Book A
ISBN 978-1-107-62704-8 Student's Book B
ISBN 978-1-107-69037-0 Workbook
ISBN 978-1-107-64988-0 Workbook A
ISBN 978-1-107-61861-9 Workbook B
ISBN 978-1-107-65940-7 Full Contact
ISBN 978-1-107-61439-0 Full Contact A
ISBN 978-1-107-66547-7 Full Contact B
ISBN 978-1-107-62402-3 Teacher's Edition with Assessment Audio CD/CD-ROM
ISBN 978-1-107-67757-9 Class Audio CDs (4)

Additional resources for this publication at www.cambridge.org/touchstone2

Contents

Making friends

Lesson A / Getting to know you

1 About you 1

Grammar and vocabulary **A** Complete the chart with the words in the box.

college	major	✓neighborhood	parents
job	movies	only child	TV

Home and family	School and work	Free time and friends
neighborhood		

B Answer the questions with your own information. Use short answers.

1. Are you an only child? _Yes, I am._ **or** _No, I'm not._
2. Is your neighborhood quiet? _____
3. Do you live with your parents? _____
4. Do you have a big TV? _____
5. Do you and your friends go to college? _____
6. Are you a French major? _____
7. Does your best friend like action movies? _____
8. Is homework fun? _____

2 You and me

Grammar Complete the conversation with the verb *be*. Use contractions where possible.

Koji Hi. ____*I'm*____ Koji.

Isabel Hi. I _____ Isabel. Where _____ you from, Koji?

Koji I _____ from Japan. How about you?

Isabel Monterrey – in Mexico.

Koji Oh, my friends Manuel and Rosa _____ from Mexico, too.

Isabel Really? _____ they here now?

Koji No, they _____ not. Uh, I guess they _____ late.

Isabel _____ the teacher here?

Koji Yes, she _____ . She _____ over there.

Isabel She looks nice. What _____ her name?

Koji I think it _____ Ms. Barnes.

3 I'm Rudy.

Grammar | Answer the questions. Write another piece of information.

1. Is Rudy from San Francisco?
   No, he's not. He's from Los Angeles.

2. Are his friends English majors?
   _____

3. Do his friends study in the evening?
   _____

4. Does Rudy live alone?
   _____

4 About you 2

Grammar and vocabulary | Unscramble the questions. Then answer the questions with your own information.

1. name / What's / first / your ? _What's your first name?_____
   _____

2. full-time / a / Do / have / you / job ? _____
   _____

3. live / best friend / Does / your / nearby ? _____
   _____

4. weekends / What / do / on / you / do ? _____
   _____

5. does / your neighbor / What / for a living / do ? _____
   _____

6. live / Do / alone / you ? _____
   _____

1 What doesn't belong?

Vocabulary | Circle the word that doesn't belong in each group.

1. apples (butter) mangoes strawberries
2. TV jacket jeans sweater
3. black color green red

4. baseball basketball singing volleyball
5. cat dog fish pet
6. dessert juice milk water

2 We're the same.

Grammar | Respond to the statements with *too* or *either*.

1. I'm a soccer fan.
   I am too.

2. I can't stand doing the laundry.
   _____

3. I can sing karaoke all night.
   _____

4. I'm not a good cook.
   _____

5. I don't like shopping.
   _____

6. I love to swim in cold water.
   _____

3 First date

Grammar and vocabulary | Complete the conversations with the expressions in the box.
You can use some expressions more than once.

> ✓ I am too.   I do too.   I can too.
> I'm not either.   I don't either.   I can't either.

David   You know, I'm always nervous on first dates.

Lesley   _I am too._____ I guess I'm not very outgoing.

David   I guess _____ So, what do you like to do in your
free time?

Lesley   Well, I go to rock concerts.

David   _____ I'm a big fan of Kings of Leon.

Lesley   _____ They're my favorite group. I mean,
I can listen to their music for hours.

David   _____ Do you have all their songs?

Lesley   No, I don't. I don't have *The End*.

David   _____ But I want to buy it.

Lesley   What do you do on the weekends? I mean, do you eat out a lot?

David   No. I don't usually go to restaurants.

Lesley   _____ I like to eat at home.

David   Oh, are you a good cook?

Lesley   Um, no. I can't say I'm a good cook.

David   _____ But I like to cook.

Lesley   Do you ever cook Italian food?

David   Sure. I love pasta and pizza.

Lesley   _____

David   That's amazing! We have a lot in common. Do you like sports?
I'm a big sports fan. I watch sports all weekend.

Lesley   Oh . . .

4 About you

Grammar and vocabulary | Respond to these statements so they are true for you.

1. A   I always eat chocolate after dinner.
   B   _I do too._ **or** _Me too._ **or** _Really? I don't._

2. A   I'm not a baseball fan.
   B   _____

3. A   I can't drive.
   B   _____

4. A   I don't have a pet.
   B   _____

5. A   I'm allergic to bananas.
   B   _____

6. A   I can cook Italian food.
   B   _____

1 Starting a conversation

Conversation strategies | **Complete the conversations with the conversation starters in the box.**

Is this your first English class here?
Hi. Are you new here? Do you live around here?
Is it me, or is it kind of noisy in here?

You look really nice today. That's a beautiful jacket.
Boy, the food is great. And this cake is really wonderful.
✓ Oh, it's cold. Can I close the window?

1. A *Oh, it's cold. Can I close the window?*
   B Sorry, I just opened it. I'm a little warm, actually.

2. A _____
   B Thanks. Actually, it's from China.

3. A _____
   B Thank you. It's my grandmother's recipe.

4. A _____
   B Yes, it is. Are you in this class, too?

5. A _____
   B Yeah, it's pretty loud! Is this your first time here?

6. A _____
   B Uh, no, I don't. I'm actually visiting from Guadalajara.

6

2 Um, actually, . . .

Conversation strategies | **Match each conversation starter with a response.**

1. It's really hot in here. __b__
2. Do you know anyone in this class? _____
3. Do you live in this neighborhood? _____
4. Do you walk to class? _____
5. I like your necklace. _____
6. Do you like coffee? _____

a. Yes, most days. It's actually only five minutes from work.

✓b. It often gets hot in here. But I feel OK today, actually.

c. No, um actually, . . . I'm a little shy.

d. Thanks. It's actually from Colombia.

e. Actually, no, but I work near here.

f. Yeah, I do. Actually, there's a great coffee shop across the street.

3 First day of class

Conversation strategies | **Imagine it's the first day of English class. Respond to each conversation starter.**

1. I don't know anyone here.   *I don't either, actually. By the way, I'm James.*

2. I feel a little nervous.

3. Is it warm in here, or is it me?

4. I don't know the teacher's name.

5. Are you a friend of Sara's?

6. I really like your bag.

7. What time does the class finish?

8. Do we get a break?

9. This is a nice classroom.

10. Can we use dictionaries, do you think?

1 Getting together

Reading **A** Read the article. Which of these are good suggestions for making small talk? Check (✓) the boxes.

☐ Don't look at the other person.
☐ Keep quiet when the other person is talking.
☐ Ask questions that start with *what*, *where*, *how*, or *when*.

☐ Have some good topics to discuss.
☐ Talk about yourself a lot.

Social Conversations

Eight Tips for Great Social Conversations

Are you shy? Do you find conversations with new people difficult? If you do, then these eight tips can help you connect. If you're outgoing and love to talk, they can help you improve your conversation skills.

1 **Have some topics ready to start a conversation.** Say something about the weather or the place you're in. Talk about the weekend – we all have something to say about weekends!

2 **Make the conversation interesting.** Know about events in the news. Read restaurant and movie reviews. Find out about the current music scene or what's new in fashion or sports.

3 **Be a good listener.** Make eye contact and say, "Yes," "Hmm," "Uh-huh," "Right," and "I know." And say, "Really? That's interesting." It encourages people to talk.

4 **Don't be boring.** Don't just say, "Yes" or "No" when you answer a question. Give some interesting details, too.

5 **Don't talk all the time.** Ask, "How about you?" and show you are interested in the other person, too. People love to talk about themselves!

6 **Ask information questions.** Ask questions like, "What do you do in your free time?" or "What kind of food do you like?" Use follow-up questions to keep the conversation going. But don't ask too many questions – it's not an interview!

7 **Be positive.** Negative comments can sound rude. And if you don't want to answer a personal question, simply say, "Oh, I'm not sure I can answer that," or "I'd rather not say."

8 **Smile!** Everyone loves a smile. Just be relaxed, smile, and be yourself.

B Read the article again and circle the correct words.

1. It's **good** / **not good** to make short responses when you listen.
2. When you answer questions, **you can say** / **don't just reply** "Yes" or "No."
3. Ask **a couple of** / **a lot of** follow-up questions.
4. **Think** / **Don't think** of a conversation like an interview.
5. You **have to** / **don't have to** answer personal questions.

2 Suggestions, please!

Writing **A Rewrite Ben's email to a magazine and the problem page editor's reply. Use correct punctuation.**

New Message

Subject: **Suggestions, please**

Dear Marcy,
i want to meet new people and make friends
the problem is that I'm shy my brother says join
a gym or a running club maybe he's right i just
hate exercise what can I do?
Ben

Dear Ben,
you need to find people with the same interests
what are your hobbies do you read a lot join a
book club think about the things you like and
find a hobby
Marcy

New Message

Subject: **Suggestions, please**

Dear Marcy,

I want to meet new people

B Read these questions. Write three suggestions for each question.

1. ***Dave*** I'd like to make friends, but I don't know how. Do you have any suggestions?

   _____

   _____

2. ***Niki*** I feel shy around new people. How can I improve my conversation skills?

   _____

   _____

Unit 1 Progress chart

What can you do? Mark the boxes. ✓ = I can . . . ? = I need to review how to . . .	To review, go back to these pages in the Student's Book.
Grammar	
☐ make statements with the simple present and present of *be*.	2, 3, 4, and 5
☐ ask questions with the simple present and present of *be*.	2 and 3
☐ use *too* and *either* to agree.	4 and 5
Vocabulary	
☐ use at least 20 words to describe home and family, school and work, and free time and friends.	2 and 3
Conversation strategies	
☐ start conversations with people I don't know.	6 and 7
☐ use *actually* to give and "correct" information.	7
Writing	
☐ use capital letters, commas, quotation marks, question marks, and periods.	9

Interests

Lesson A / Leisure time

 1 What do they like to do?

Grammar | **Complete the sentences. Use the correct form of the verbs in the box.
Sometimes there is more than one correct answer.**

| cook | dance | draw | play | ✓read | work out |

1. Pam and Victor aren't interested in _reading_ books. They both prefer _to read_ magazines. They really enjoy _reading_ fashion magazines.

2. Ian would like _____ every day. He doesn't like _____ in the gym. He enjoys _____ at home.

3. Sun Hee can't _____ . She's interested in _____ and would like _____ the tango.

4. Tom isn't good at _____ people. He hates _____ people, but he can _____ animals very well.

5. Amy and Dave usually like _____ , but they can't _____ Italian food. They prefer _____ Chinese food.

6. Erica can't _____ the guitar very well. She enjoys _____ music, but she's not very good at _____ it.

2 At home

Grammar | Complete the sentences. Use the correct form of the verbs in the box. Sometimes there is more than one correct answer.

bowl	go	ski	try
✓exercise	play	swim	watch

Linda You and I watch too much TV. We need some exercise.

James I know, but I don't really enjoy _exercising_ .

Linda But you like _____ tennis, right?

James Yeah, but these days I prefer _____ tennis on TV.

Linda How about bowling? You're good at _____ .

James Yeah, but it's always noisy at the bowling alley.

Linda I guess you're right.

James Well, we can both _____ . And the pool's nearby.

Linda But it's always crowded.

James Oh, I know! We both like _____ .

Linda Actually, I can't stand the cold and snow.

James Really? Well, are you interested in _____ something new?

Linda Sure. I'd like _____ to the new Thai restaurant in our neighborhood.

James Great idea, Linda. Let's think about exercising tomorrow.

3 About you

Grammar and vocabulary | Answer the questions with true information. Add more information.

1. A What are you good at?

   B _Well, I'm pretty good at learning languages. I can speak Portuguese and French._

2. A What are you bad at?

   B _____

3. A Would you like to play a musical instrument?

   B _____

4. A What movie do you want to see?

   B _____

5. A What do you really hate doing?

   B _____

6. A What do you enjoy doing on the weekends?

   B _____

1 All kinds of music

Vocabulary Look at the pictures. Write the type of music.

1. __folk music__   2. j_____   3. r_____   4. l_____

5. c_____   6. c_____   7. p_____   8. r_____

2 What's new?

Grammar Complete Kevin's email with the correct words.

New Message		

To: Sam_P@cup.com
From: KevinJ@cup.com
Subject: My new job

Hi Sam,

Guess what! I have a new job at a café. They play some great music here so it's a great job for
____me____ (me / it). I really like _____ (him / it).

They play music by some great bands, like Maroon 5. Do you know _____ (her / them)? Then there's Bruno Mars. He's cool. I really like _____ (him / it), too. Actually, I think almost everybody in the café _____ (is / are) a Bruno Mars fan. Do you like country music? I don't really care for _____ (it / him). No one I know really _____ (like / likes) country. But I think Taylor Swift is cool, and she has a great new album. Do you know _____ (us / her)?

Oh, did I tell you? I'm in a band with some friends at the café. They're really great. I want you to meet _____ (him / them). We play hip-hop. But no one in my family _____ (come / comes) to listen to _____ (him / us). They don't like hip-hop! But that's OK.

What's new with you? Write soon.

Kevin

3 Talking about music

Grammar | **Complete the questions with object pronouns. Then answer the questions.**

1. A Beyoncé's a great singer. She's pretty, too.
   Do you like ___*her*___ ?
   B *Yes, I do. She's amazing.*

2. A You know Justin Timberlake, right? I think he's great.
   What do you think of _____ ?
   B _____

3. A You know, I'm not a fan of jazz. How about you?
   Do you ever listen to _____ ?
   B _____

4. A Hey, the Black Keys were on TV last night. They're a really
   cool band. Do you know _____ ?
   B _____

5. A My mom and dad love Sarah Chang. She's their favorite
   violinist. Do your parents like _____ ?
   B _____

6. A Do you like Latin music? Jeff and I have tickets for the Shakira
   concert. Do you want to go with _____ ?
   B _____

7. A I don't usually like country bands, but I love Lady Antebellum.
   Do you know _____ ?
   B _____

4 About you

 | **Answer the questions using object pronouns. Then give more information.**

1. Do you like Alicia Keys? *Yes, I like her a lot. She has some great songs.* **or**
   Actually, I don't know her.

2. What do you think of the Rolling Stones? _____

3. Do you like Mariah Carey? _____

4. Do you listen to pop music very often? _____

5. What do you think of folk music? _____

6. Do you and your friends ever go to concerts? _____

7. What do you think of Bruno Mars? _____

8. Do you know the band The Lumineers? _____

13

1 Saying no

Conversation strategies — Complete the conversations with the sentences in the box.

> Not really. He just watches TV a lot. ✓ Not really. My mom knitted it for me last year.
> Actually, no. My sister got it at the bakery. No, but he collects caps.
> Well, no. I like to make peanut butter cookies. No. I'm not really good with my hands.
> Um, no. He just uses it for computer games. Not really. Well, I guess his computer is a hobby.

1. Jenny   I really like your sweater. Is it new?

    Keiko   *Not really. My mom knitted it for me last year.*

    Jenny   It's really nice. So, can you knit, too?

    Keiko   _____ But I bake a little.

    Jenny   Oh, did you make this cake?

    Keiko   _____

            But I like to make cookies sometimes.

    Jenny   Me too. Do you ever make chocolate chip cookies?

    Keiko   _____

            My new boyfriend loves them!

2. Mike   I want to buy a Yankees baseball cap for my brother.

    Greg   Why? Is it his birthday?

    Mike   _____

           Does your brother collect anything?

    Greg   My brother? _____

    Mike   But he can't watch it all the time. Does he have any
           hobbies?

    Greg   _____

    Mike   Oh, yeah? My brother is on the computer all the time.

    Greg   Oh, does he use it for homework?

    Mike   _____

2 No, not really.

Conversation strategies — Complete the responses to make them more friendly.

1. A Do you go online a lot?

   B Not really. *I don't have a computer.*

2. A What a great photo! Are you interested
      in photography?

   B No. _____

3. A I really enjoy my piano lessons. Would
      you like to learn to play the piano?

   B Um, no. _____

4. A I love growing flowers and vegetables. Do
      you enjoy gardening?

   B Well, not really. _____

3 Yes and no

Conversation strategies | Answer the questions in a friendly way. Use *really* in each answer.

1. A Are you good at fixing things?
   B No, *not really. I'm not good with my hands* .
   C Yes, *I'm really good at fixing cars* .

2. A Do you make your own clothes?
   B No, _____ .
   C Yes, _____ .

3. A Does your best friend collect anything?
   B No, _____ .
   C Yes, _____ .

4. A Does your teacher speak Russian?
   B No, _____ .
   C Yes, _____ .

5. A Are you into winter sports, like skiing?
   B No, _____ .
   C Yes, _____ .

6. A Do you and your friends enjoy cooking?
   B Um, no, _____ .
   C Yes, _____ .

7. A Are your classmates into computer games?
   B No, _____ .
   C Yes, _____ .

8. A Are you interested in photography?
   B No, _____ .
   C Yes, _____ .

4 About you

Conversation strategies | Answer the questions with your own information. Use *really* in your answers.

1. Are you into sports?

   Yes, I really like soccer and volleyball. **or**
   No, not really. I prefer doing artistic things.

2. Would you like to learn a new language?

   _____

3. Do you have a lot of hobbies?

   _____

4. Can you knit or sew?

   _____

5. Are you artistic?

   _____

1 Popular interests

Reading **A** Read the online forum posts. Write the correct topic for each post.

✓Cooking   Music   Photography   Running   Water sports
Fashion   Pets   Reading   Technology   Winter sports

Denver Hobby Forum

► ___Cooking___

From: sushifreak
I want to learn how to make Japanese food, especially sushi. Do you have any easy recipe ideas?

► _____

From: ladiva
I enjoy singing, and I want to start a jazz band. I'm looking for piano and trumpet players. Please email me at ladiva@cup.org.

► _____

From: trailblazer
I just started running. I really want to run a marathon. Can anyone suggest good places to train in the city?

► _____

From: sunriser
I love to take pictures, especially sunrises. Does anyone know a good place to take pictures? I'd prefer a place that's close to my house, if possible.

► _____

From: grungeking
I want to find a good place for vintage clothes in Portland, Maine. I also want to buy shoes and accessories. Any ideas?

► _____

From: teacher
I love using apps for just about everything. I want to create my own app to help people learn Spanish. Can anyone recommend a good company for building apps?

► _____

From: snowthrills
I'm good at skiing, and I'd like to try snowboarding. Can anyone suggest a good teacher?

► _____

From: heartbroken
We have a beautiful gray cat – free to a good home in the New York area. We can't keep her because I just found out I'm allergic to cats.

B Read the responses to the posts below. Who are they for? Match the responses with the writers of the posts. Write *a* to *h*.

1. I like to run the track at Livingston Park. __c__
2. IceCat Technology makes good software. ____
3. I'm pretty good at playing the piano. Let's jam! ____
4. We'd love to have her! We live in Bergen County. ____
5. I take pictures at Keystone Park. It has great views. ____
6. Try www.50s.cup.com. They have great 1950s dresses and stuff. ____
7. I can send you my recipe for *kayu*. It's delicious! ____
8. Call the ski resort and ask for an experienced instructor. ____

a. teacher
b. heartbroken
✓c. trailblazer
d. snowthrills
e. sushifreak
f. ladiva
g. sunriser
h. grungeking

2 My favorite hobby

Writing **A** Complete the post with *and*, *but*, *or*, *also*, *because*, or *especially*. Sometimes there is more than one correct answer.

Message Board   ⬚ 🗗 ✕

Rock climbing

One of my hobbies is rock climbing. I go once or twice a month with my family ____*or*____ friends. We like to climb the mountains near my house _____ they're really beautiful _____ the views are wonderful. We often go to Bear Mountain _____ Kennedy Park. I prefer Kennedy Park _____ it's closer. Kennedy Park _____ has a great campground.

It's great to be outdoors, _____ the weather isn't always very good. When it's raining _____ snowing, climbing can be very dangerous _____ the rocks get wet and slippery.

In the winter, my friends _____ I sometimes go rock climbing indoors, usually on a Saturday _____ Sunday. There's a climbing wall at the mall, _____ it's not the same. We prefer to be outdoors, _____ in the summer.

B Write about one of your hobbies.

One of my hobbies is

Unit 2 Progress chart

What can you do? Mark the boxes. ☑ = I can . . . ? = I need to review how to . . .	To review, go back to these pages in the Student's Book.
Grammar ⬚ make statements with different verb forms.	12 and 13
⬚ ask questions with different verb forms.	12 and 13
⬚ use the correct verb forms after other verbs, modal verbs, and prepositions.	12 and 13
⬚ use object pronouns, and the pronouns *everybody* and *nobody*.	15
Vocabulary ⬚ name at least 8 common interests.	12 and 13
⬚ name at least 8 hobbies.	12, 13, 16, and 17
⬚ name at least 8 kinds of music.	14 and 15
Conversation strategies ⬚ say *no* in a polite and friendly way.	16 and 17
⬚ use *really* and *not really* to make statements stronger or softer.	17
Writing ⬚ use *and*, *but*, *or*, *also*, *especially*, or *because* to link ideas.	19

Health

Lesson A / Healthy living

1 Staying in shape

Grammar | Complete the conversations with the correct form of the verbs.

1. **Max**   Hi, Carl. How ___is___ it _going_ (go)?

   Carl   Great. What _____ you _____ (do)?

   Max   Oh. I _____ (try) to get in shape before graduation.

   Carl   So _____ you _____ (try) to lose weight?

   Max   Yeah, a little. I _____ (want) to look good in the photo.
   So this month I _____ (exercise) and _____ (eat) salads.
   And I _____ (cut) down on fried food and things like that.

   Carl   Good for you. You know, I _____ (read) an interesting book
   about healthy eating right now. _____ you _____ (want)
   to borrow it?

   Max   Sure. Thanks. But you always _____ (look) so good.
   You _____ (not need) to lose weight.

   Carl   Well, it's probably because I usually _____ (eat) healthy
   foods and I _____ (exercise) most days.

2. **Doctor**   So, Paul, you _____ (want) to improve your lifestyle.

   Paul   Yes, I _____ (need) to get into shape. I know I _____ (not get)
   enough exercise right now, but I _____ (not have) the energy.

   Doctor   So, what exercise _____ you _____ (do) these days?

   Paul   Actually, I _____ (not get) any exercise at all. I _____ (work)
   on a big project for my job, and I _____ (not have) a lot of time.
   Life's kind of stressful right now.

   Doctor   So how _____ you usually _____ (cope) with stress?

   Paul   Well, right now, I _____ (not cope) really. Usually I _____ (not eat)
   a lot of snacks and chocolate, but I _____ (eat) a lot of them now.

   Doctor   So _____ you usually _____ (have) a healthy diet?

   Paul   Well, it's not bad, I guess. I _____ (love) red meat, and I _____ (eat)
   that every day. I _____ really _____ (not like) vegetables, so
   I _____ often _____ (not eat) them.

   Doctor   Well, I think you _____ (need) to eat a balanced diet and to get more exercise.
   Try this plan for four weeks. Then come back in two weeks so we can review it.

   Paul   OK. Thanks.

2 Susan's lifestyle

Grammar | Look at the picture and complete the email with the correct form of the verbs in the box.

| do | drink | drink | eat | have | not buy | not do | not try | play | want | ✓ work out |

New Message

To: Cassie_90_P@cup.com
From: Marcy@cup.com
Subject: My new roommate

Hey Cassie. Do you want to meet my new roommate? You'd like her. She is SO healthy. I'm writing emails, and she _'s working out_ on her new exercise bike. She _____ to lose weight or anything, but she says that she _____ to stay healthy. And look – she _____ water, too! I mean, I _____ soda – but not her! She _____ a pretty healthy diet and lifestyle. She _____ a lot of fruit, and she _____ much junk food. Usually, she _____ tennis once a month, but now she _____ karate twice a week, too. I really need to do something like that. I _____ anything to stay healthy. :)

---

3 About you

Grammar and vocabulary | Are these sentences true or false for you? Write *T* (true) or *F* (false). Then correct the false statements.

1. __F__ I'm drinking a lot of milk these days.
   I'm not drinking a lot of milk these days. I'm drinking a lot of soda.

2. _____ My best friend eats junk food every day.
   _____

3. _____ I'm not taking any classes right now.
   _____

4. _____ I sleep for five hours a night.
   _____

5. _____ My friends have a lot of stress in their lives.
   _____

6. _____ My family doesn't get any exercise at all.
   _____

1 What's the matter?

Vocabulary **A** There are seven health problems in the puzzle. Find the other six.
Look in these directions (→ ↓).

A	T	O	O	T	H	A	C	H	E	W	A
B	C	K	F	M	U	U	O	E	R	F	L
S	O	R	E	T	H	R	O	A	T	D	L
R	U	I	V	D	E	I	H	D	U	J	E
V	G	J	P	L	A	R	U	P	L	A	F
E	H	C	S	H	E	A	D	A	C	H	E
S	I	O	T	B	J	W	L	S	A	N	V
O	H	L	F	O	V	A	O	U	B	D	E
B	E	A	L	L	E	R	G	I	E	S	R
G	A	N	G	D	C	K	S	W	N	C	H
S	T	O	M	A	C	H	A	C	H	E	I
R	M	R	L	T	N	F	R	G	C	S	R

B Look at the picture. Write sentences with the words from part A.

Joe   Taro   Chad   Amy   Jim and Liz   Sara   Joyce

1. _Joe has a fever._

2. _____

3. _____

4. _____

5. _____

6. _____

7. _____

2 I feel sick.

Grammar
and
vocabulary | **Look at the pictures. Write questions and answers.**

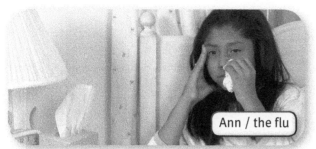

Ann / the flu

Dan / a cold

1. _What does Ann do when she has the flu?_

    When _Ann has the flu, she stays in bed_ .

2. _____

    If _____ .

Rick / a headache

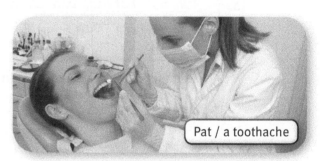

Pat / a toothache

3. _____

    _____ when _____ .

4. _____

    _____ if_____ .

3 About you

Grammar
and
vocabulary | **Write questions for a friend using *when* or *if*. Then answer your friend's questions.**

1. You   _What do you do when you're sick?_ _____
    (when / are sick)

    Friend   When I'm sick, I stay home and watch movies all day. How about you?

    You   _____

2. You   _____
    (if / have a bad cough)

    Friend   I usually take cough medicine if I have a bad cough. What do you do?

    You   _____

3. You   _____
    (if / get an upset stomach)

    Friend   If I get an upset stomach, I drink water. I don't eat a lot. How about you?

    You   _____

4. You   _____
    (when / have a fever)

    Friend   When I have a fever, I take aspirin and I don't go out. What about you?

    You   _____

1 It's my allergies.

Conversation strategies

Complete the conversation. Use the sentences in the box.

> Are you serious? How come? I mean, why not?
> ✓ Oh, no! That's too bad. Do you sneeze a lot?
> You're kidding! So you never take medicine?
> Headaches? Do you take anything?
>
> Gosh, that's terrible! So, what are you studying?
> Really? So how do you study when you don't
>   feel good?

Joan   Gary, are you OK? Your eyes are all red.

Gary   Oh, it's my allergies. I always feel this way in the spring.

Joan   *Oh, no! That's too bad. Do you sneeze a lot?*

Gary   Yeah. I sneeze all the time. And I get headaches, too.

Joan   _____

Gary   Not really. Actually, I don't like to take medicine.

Joan   _____

Gary   No. Never. And especially allergy medicine. If I take it, I can't study.

Joan   _____

Gary   Well, you see, when I take medicine, I always fall asleep.

Joan   _____

Gary   It's hard, but I have to try. Right now I'm studying for a big test next week.

Joan   _____

Gary   I'm studying medicine!

2 You're kidding!

Conversation strategies

Circle the best response to show surprise.

1. My husband talks in his sleep.
   a. My husband does, too.
   b. Wow! What does he say?

2. I love getting up early on weekends.
   a. Do you get up early on weekdays, too?
   b. Are you serious? On weekends?

3. I take two or three naps every day.
   a. Gosh! Do you sleep OK at night?
   b. I know. I saw you fall asleep in class once!

4. I often drink hot chocolate if I can't sleep.
   a. Me too. I love hot chocolate at night.
   b. You're kidding! It keeps me awake.

5. My grandmother goes running six days a week.
   a. No way! How old is she?
   b. So she's really into exercise, huh?

6. I often dream about food.
   a. I do too. I always dream about ice cream.
   b. Really? Are you hungry when you go to bed?

7. I have three part-time jobs.
   a. Oh, wow! You work really hard.
   b. Do you often get tired?

8. If I can't sleep, I often listen to rock music.
   a. Gosh! I can't sleep with music on.
   b. Me too. I also listen to pop music.

3 No way!

Conversation strategies **Write responses to show surprise. Then ask follow-up questions.**

1. A One of my friends cleans the house when he can't sleep.
   B _No way!_   _So does he go back to bed at all?_

2. A My best friend remembers all her dreams.
   B _____ _____

3. A I sometimes sleep at the office.
   B _____ _____

4. A Sometimes I can't sleep because my neighbors play loud music.
   B _____ _____

5. A My little brother has the same nightmare about once a month.
   B _____ _____

6. A My father sleepwalks every night.
   B _____ _____

7. A I never use an alarm clock.
   B _____ _____

8. A My sister goes running right after she eats dinner.
   B _____ _____

4 About you

Conversation strategies **Answer the questions with your own information.**

1. Are you feeling sleepy right now? _____

2. How often do you take naps on weekdays? _____

3. Do you ever sleep in class or at work? _____

4. Are you sleeping well these days? _____

5. What do you do when you wake up at night? _____

6. Do you dream in color? _____

1 Understanding stress

Reading | **A** Read the leaflet. Which of these are signs of stress? Check (✓) the boxes.

☐ You have health problems.   ☐ You are tired.
☐ You can't concentrate.   ☐ You breathe slowly.
☐ You have a lot of energy.   ☐ You feel irritable.

Common Questions About Stress

Am I stressed?
If you can't sleep well or can't concentrate, . . .
If you feel depressed or want to cry a lot, . . .
If you have a headache or an upset stomach, . . .
If you can't relax and you feel irritable, . . .
If you are extremely tired, . . .

   . . . then it's possible you are stressed.

Is stress bad for me?
Occasional stress is common and not always
bad for you. However, if you feel stressed
for a long time, it can be serious. Stress can
make you sick. It can also affect your memory
or concentration, so it's hard to get your
work done.

What can I do?
Fortunately, there's a lot you can do. Try some
of these relaxation techniques. If you still feel
stressed, then make an appointment to see
your doctor.

Relaxation Techniques

1. **Breathe** Take a breath, hold it for four
   seconds, and then breathe out very slowly.
   Feel your body relax.
2. **Exercise** Walk or exercise for just 30 minutes
   each day and feel better.

3. **Talk** Call a friend. Talk about your problems.
4. **Meditate** Close your eyes and focus on
   something calm. Feel relaxed.
5. **Pamper yourself** Take a hot bath, or have
   a massage.

6. **Do something you enjoy** Listen to music.
   Sing. Watch TV. Meet a friend for coffee.

Department of Health – "Take care of yourself."

B Read the leaflet again. Then choose the correct words to complete the sentences.

1. When you're stressed, it's not easy to ___relax___ .   a. relax   b. cry
2. Stress _____ a lot of people.   a. affects   b. doesn't affect
3. Stress is _____ good for you.   a. sometimes   b. never
4. If you're very stressed, you often can't _____ .   a. exercise   b. think
5. One good relaxation technique is to _____ .   a. see a doctor b. take a bath

2 Healthy lifestyles

Writing **A** Read these suggestions for a healthy lifestyle. Add commas where necessary.

Healthy Habits

BY DR. GOODMAN

Take yoga classes. When you practice yoga, you stay in shape and relax at the same time.

If you can't sleep drink a glass of warm milk.

Sing at home or in your car if you want to have a lot of energy.

When you listen to music choose relaxing music.

If you feel sad take a long walk. Exercise can help your mood.

Do something you love when life is stressful.

B Choose one of the titles below and write a short article. Give three suggestions.

Sleep	Food and Diet	Exercise

Unit 3 Progress chart

What can you do? Mark the boxes. ✓ = I can . . . ? = I need to review how to . . .	To review, go back to these pages in the Student's Book.
Grammar	
☐ make statements with the simple present and present continuous.	22 and 23
☐ ask questions with the simple present and present continuous.	22 and 23
☐ use *if* and *when* in statements and questions.	25
Vocabulary	
☐ name at least 8 healthy habits.	22 and 23
☐ name at least 4 unhealthy habits.	22 and 23
☐ name at least 6 health problems.	24 and 25
Conversation strategies	
☐ keep a conversation going with comments and follow-up questions.	26 and 27
☐ use expressions like *Wow!* or *You're kidding!* to show surprise.	27
Writing	
☐ use commas in *if* and *when* clauses.	29

25

Celebrations

Lesson **A** / **Birthdays**

1 What month is it?

Vocabulary **A** Write the months in the correct order.

1. _____January_____   4. _____   7. _____   10. _____

2. _____   5. _____   8. _____   11. _____

3. _____   6. _____   9. _____   12. _____

B Complete the sentences with the correct numbers.

1. January is the ____first____ month of the year.

2. March is the _____ month of the year.

3. June is the _____ month of the year.

4. July is the _____ month of the year.

5. October is the _____ month of the year.

6. December is the _____ month of the year.

2 When's her birthday?

Grammar
and
vocabulary Look at the dates. Then write each person's birthday two ways.

1. _Halle Berry's birthday is on August fourteenth._
   Her birthday is on the fourteenth of August.

2. _____
   _____

3. _____
   _____

4. _____
   _____

5. _____
   _____

6. _____
   _____

❶

❷

Halle Berry 8/14

Jackie Chan 4/7

❸

❹

Justin Timberlake 1/31

Emily Blunt 2/23

❺

❻

Jennifer Lopez 7/24

Fernando Torres 3/20

3 Future plans

Grammar | **Complete the conversations with the correct form of _be going to_.**

1. Sam What _are you going to do_ (you / do) this weekend?

    Diane I _____ (see) my grandmother. We _____ (have) a birthday party for her.

    Sam That's nice. How _____ (you / celebrate)? I mean, _____ (it / be) a big party?

    Diane No, not really. We _____ (not do) much. It _____ (be) just the family. Mom _____ (bake) her a cake. Then her friends _____ (take) her dancing. She's a tango teacher.

    Sam Your grandmother's a tango teacher? Cool.

2. Yumi That was Jun on the phone. He can't take us to Sarah's party.

    Kara Oh, no. Why not?

    Yumi No car. His parents _____ (go) away this weekend, and they _____ (take) the car.

    Kara Huh. Where _____ (they / go)? Well, anyway, _____ Dan _____ (be) there?

    Yumi Yeah, but he _____ (not go) until after work.

    Kara Well, it looks like we _____ (have to) walk. Wear comfortable shoes!

4 Happy birthday!

Grammar and vocabulary | **Complete the card. Put the words in order.**

Dear Kathleen,

Happy birthday! I'm sending you this card
(sending / this / you / card / I'm) from Mexico. Hector and I are in Mexico City; we're visiting his parents.
_____ (us / all the sights / showing / 're / They). His mother Beatriz is so nice.
_____ (some / I / her / jewelry / brought) from New York, and she wears it everywhere.

_____ (me / is / Beatriz / teaching / Spanish) and how to make Mexican food. She says _____ (to / get / she / going / us / 's) a tamale pot to take home. Hector loves tamales, and _____ (tamales / want to / him / make / I) on special occasions. We want to take his parents to a nice restaurant, but _____ (dinner / can / them / we / buy / never). They never let us pay for anything!

Anyway, how about you? _____
(I / Can / you / bring / anything) from Mexico for your birthday?

Ellen

1 Good times

Vocabulary | **Look at the pictures. Write the special event. Then complete the descriptions with the expressions in the box.**

blow out (the) candle	go out for a romantic dinner	shout "Happy New Year"
exchange rings	go trick-or-treating	sing "Happy Birthday"
get a diploma	have a reception	✓ wear a cap and gown
give her chocolates	see the fireworks	wear costumes

graduation day

1. Ana and her classmates have to _wear a cap and gown_ . When they call her name, Ana's going to _____ .

_____

2. The waiters _____ when they bring out a cake. Erin's going to make a wish and _____ .

_____

3. Allen and Carine decided to _____ . After dinner, Allen's going to _____ .

_____

4. Bruce and Sheila are at a big party on the beach. They wanted to _____ . At midnight, they're going to _____ .

_____

5. Ahmad and Keisha are getting married. During the wedding, they're going to _____ . After the wedding, they're going to _____ .

_____

6. John and Blake love to _____ of their favorite comic-book characters. When they're ready, they're going to _____ in the neighborhood.

2 A busy week

Grammar | **Read George's calendar. Write a sentence about each plan. Use the present continuous.**

MAY

Sunday	Monday	Tuesday	Wednesday	Thursday	Friday	Saturday
8	9	10	11	12	13	14
Mother's Day – have lunch with Mom	**8:00** – Meet Ann for dinner	Play tennis with Greg after work	**8:00** – See a movie with Joe	Work out with Dan before work	**2:00** – Give a speech at Keith and Karen's wedding	**5:00** – Go to Jennifer's graduation party

1. _On May eighth, George is having lunch with his mother._
2. _____
3. _____
4. _____
5. _____
6. _____
7. _____

3 What's going to happen?

Grammar | **Write a prediction about each picture. Use *be going to*. Some are negative.**

1. _It's going to rain._
   (rain)

2. _____
   (go trick-or-treating)

3. _____
   (give / flowers)

4. _____
   (see / fireworks)

5. _____
   (get a diploma)

6. _____
   (be sunny)

1 "Vague" expressions

Rewrite the underlined words, if possible, using vague expressions like *and everything*, *and stuff (like that)*, or *and things (like that)*. You can't rewrite some of them.

1. Maya   Let's do something different this year for New Year's. Like take a vacation.

   Jake   OK. We work hard, <u>and I think we really need a break</u>.

   Maya   Yes, I'd like to go away on vacation and lie on a beach and read *and stuff* ~~and relax and sleep~~.

   Jake   Yeah, and then in the evenings we can have some nice romantic dinners with candles <u>and music and nice food</u>.

   Maya   Or we can go to movies and concerts <u>and listen to local bands and singers</u>.

   Jake   Could you give me my tablet? We can look online, <u>and I'm sure we can find a nice place to go</u>.

   Maya   Just one thing. Who's going to tell everyone, <u>especially your parents</u>, that we're not going to be at the family party this year?

2. Sonia   Hey, there's a Rodeo Days festival today <u>and tomorrow</u>. What is it exactly?

   Pete   Well, every February <u>they have this festival</u>, and all the kids dress up in cowboy costumes with cowboy boots <u>and hats and scarves</u>. And they ride horses, and there's a parade <u>and competitions and exhibits</u>. So what do you think? Do you want to go?

   Sonia   Maybe. I don't know, I'm not big on rodeos <u>and cowboys and horses</u>.

   Pete   Well, it's really kind of fun. And people sell jewelry and T-shirts <u>and belts and boots and hats</u>.

   Sonia   Well, that sounds fun.

   Pete   And they have cowboy food like beans <u>and steak and other kinds of cowboy food</u>.

   Sonia   Oh, OK. So let's go – <u>maybe this afternoon</u>?

2 About you

Conversation strategies Answer the questions with the responses in the box. Use each response only once. Then add more information.

✓I don't know.   I'm not sure.   It depends.   Maybe.

1. Are you going to celebrate your birthday with a party and everything?

   I don't know. My girlfriend usually surprises me on my birthday.

2. What do you want to do this weekend?

   _____

3. Are you going to send your mother some flowers on her birthday?

   _____

4. Do you want to go see the fireworks tonight?

   _____

3 Scrambled conversation

Conversation strategies Number the lines of the conversation in the correct order.

☐ But you can also shop for cool Chinese gifts and things.

1 Would you like to go to a Chinese festival?

☐ Well, maybe. What do people do?

☐ There's going to be free food? Great, I'd love to go.

☐ Well, I don't know. I'm not big on dances and stuff like that.

☐ Well, at least the food is great, and it's free.

☐ Uh, maybe, but I don't have money for shopping right now.

☐ It's for Chinese New Year.

☐ Lots of things, like lion dances, fireworks, and everything!

☐ I'm not sure. What kind of festival is it exactly?

1 Celebrating mothers

Reading **A** Read the article. Then add the correct heading to each paragraph.

History of the holiday
Ideas for Mother's Day
Traditional ways to celebrate

When is Mother's Day?
✓ Why people celebrate Mother's Day

Mother's Day

Why people celebrate Mother's Day

In many countries, there is a special day of the year when children of all ages celebrate their mothers. On this day – Mother's Day – children tell their mothers that they love them, and thank them for their love and care.

_____

Mother's Day is not a new celebration. Historians say that it started as a spring festival in ancient Greece. The modern festival of Mother's Day probably comes from England in the 1600s, when people had a day off from their jobs to visit their mothers on a day they called "Mothering Sunday." They took small gifts and a special cake called "simnel cake." In the United States, Mother's Day became an official holiday in 1914.

_____

People in different countries celebrate Mother's Day on different days. In Spain and Portugal, Mother's Day is the first Sunday in May. In Australia, Brazil, Italy, Japan, Turkey, and the United States, it's on the second Sunday in May,

whereas in France and Sweden, it's on the last Sunday in May. In Argentina, Mother's Day is celebrated on the third Sunday in October.

_____

Although many countries celebrate Mother's Day at different times of the year, the holidays have one purpose in common – to show love and appreciation for mothers. For example, on Mother's Day morning, some children give their mothers gifts they made especially for this holiday.

_____

What are you going to do next Mother's Day? Maybe you can use some of these ideas to make your mother feel special.

- _Make or buy your mother a beautiful Mother's Day card_
- _Write her a letter telling her why you appreciate her_
- _Make her a special meal or bake a cake_
- _Plant a flower or tree somewhere she can see it_

B Read the article again. Answer the questions.

1. Where did the idea of Mother's Day come from originally? _It came from ancient Greece._

2. Which country started the tradition of giving presents on Mother's Day? _____

3. What was Mother's Day called in England? _____

4. When do Brazil and Japan celebrate Mother's Day? _____

5. What do you do on Mother's Day? _____

2 Making plans

Writing **A** Start and end these notes to different people.

An email to a friend

To: steve_P@cup.com
Subject: MY PARTY

Hi Steve,

I'm having a party on
Saturday night. Everybody's
going to be there. Hope you
can make it.

See you then.

A note to your neighbor

_____

*I'm having a party on
Friday. We're going to
have a band. I hope
it's not too noisy.
Please join us.*

_____

An email to your teacher

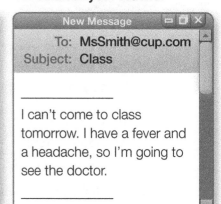

To: MsSmith@cup.com
Subject: Class

_____

I can't come to class
tomorrow. I have a fever and
a headache, so I'm going to
see the doctor.

_____

B Write to these people about a special celebration.

An email to a teacher

To:
Subject:

A note to a friend

An email to your grandparents

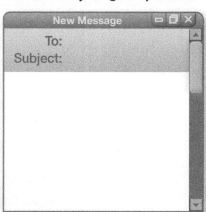

To:
Subject:

Unit 4 Progress chart

What can you do? Mark the boxes. ☑ = I can . . . ? = I need to review how to . . .	To review, go back to these pages in the Student's Book.
Grammar ☐ use *be going to* for the future.	35, 36, and 37
☐ use indirect objects and indirect object pronouns.	34 and 35
☐ use the present continuous for specific future plans.	37
Vocabulary ☐ say dates with the months of the year and ordinal numbers.	34
☐ describe things people do on holidays and special days.	34
Conversation strategies ☐ use "vague" expressions like *and everything* and *and things*.	38 and 39
☐ use "vague" responses like *I don't know* and *Maybe*.	39
Writing ☐ start and end invitations, emails, and personal notes.	41

Growing up

Lesson A / Childhood

1 What's the year?

Vocabulary | Write the years in numbers or words.

1. twenty ten _____2010_____
2. nineteen oh-four _____
3. two thousand eight _____
4. nineteen seventy-seven _____

5. 1982 _____nineteen eighty-two_____
6. 2006 _____
7. 2013 _____
8. 1998 _____

2 Talking about the past

Grammar | Complete the conversations with *was*, *wasn't*, *were*, *weren't*, *did*, or *didn't*.

1. **Rick** So, Dina, ____*did*____ you grow up here in Miami?

    Dina Yes, I _____ , but we _____ born here. My sister
    and I _____ born in Puerto Rico, and we moved here
    when we _____ kids.

    Rick So, _____ you study English when you _____ in
    school in Puerto Rico?

    Dina Yes, we _____ – for a few years – but we _____ really
    learn English until we came here.

    Rick Wow! And now you speak English better than I do – and
    I _____ born here!

2. **Thomas** When ____*were*____ you born, Grandma?

    Grandma I _____ born in 1934.

    Thomas Really? _____ you born here in Los Angeles?

    Grandma No, I _____ . Your grandfather and I _____
    both born in China.

    Thomas So when _____ you come to the U.S.?

    Grandma My family _____ move here until I _____ 13 years old.

    Thomas Really? So _____ you sad to leave all your friends
    and family in China?

    Grandma Yes, we _____ . But we _____ sad for long. We soon made friends and everything.

    Thomas That's good. When _____ Grandpa born?

    Grandma He _____ born in 1933, but he says he _____ really born until 1952.

    Thomas Why does he say that?

    Grandma Because that's when he met *me*!

3 A life story

Grammar | **Complete the story with the words in the box. You can use some words more than once.**

| ✓ago | for | from | in | last | long | then | to | until | when |

This is a picture of my best friend, Mi-young. I took it a few years ___ago___.
Mi-young and I met _____ 1994. We were very young _____ we
became friends. Mi-young is a very interesting person. She was born in Busan,
South Korea, _____ 1990. Her family moved to the U.S. _____ she was
three years old. They lived in Chicago _____ Mi-young was 15.
_____ they moved to New York City. I cried _____ a long time after
they moved.

Mi-young didn't live in New York _____ because she came back to Chicago
for college _____ she was 18. We were roommates at the University of Chicago _____
four years – _____ 2008 _____ 2012. We graduated and shared an apartment _____ a few
months. _____ she got a great job in Phoenix, Arizona, and moved there. I really missed her, but
guess what? _____ month she called and said there's a perfect job for me at her company. So I'm
going there _____ October for an interview, and I can't wait!

4 About you

Grammar and vocabulary | **Write questions using the prompts given. Then answer the questions with your own information.**

1. When / you born ? _When were you born?_____

   _____

2. Where / your parents born ? _____

   _____

3. Where / you grow up ? _____

   _____

4. Who / your best friend five years ago ? _____

   _____

5. you / ever move when you were a child ? _____

   _____

6. you / play outside a lot when you were little ? _____

   _____

7. How old / you when you started school ? _____

   _____

1 What's the subject?

A Cross out the word that doesn't belong. Then write the general category of the subjects.

1. history   ~~chemistry~~   economics   geography   *social studies*

2. gymnastics   dance   art   track   _____

3. geometry   computer studies   algebra   calculus   _____

4. literature   biology   chemistry   physics   _____

5. choir   band   drama   orchestra   _____

B Complete the crossword puzzle.

1.a	l	2.g	e	b	r	3.a			
							4.		5.
			6.						
	7.								
					8.				
	9.								
10.									

Across

1. This is one subject in math.
7. Students run short and long distances in this P.E. class.
8. Students learn to sing in this music class.
9. In this subject, students study about people and events from a long time ago.
10. Students learn to be actors when they study this subject.

Down

2. In this class, students study countries of the world and natural features, populations, and climate.
3. Students draw and paint in this class.
4. This subject is a science. Students learn about plant and animal life.
5. In this subject, teachers ask students to read novels, stories, and poems.
6. In this class, students play classical music on instruments.

2 How did we do?

Grammar **A** Write the determiners in order in the chart below.

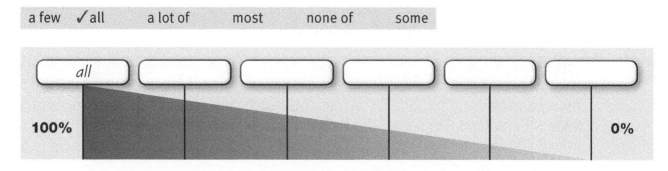

a few ✓ all   a lot of   most   none of   some

| all | | | | | |

100%   0%

B Read the test results. Then complete the sentences with the words in the box and add *of* where necessary. Some expressions are used more than once.

	A	B	C	D	E
1		Chemistry	English	Geography	Geometry
2	**Passed**	55%	100%	90%	15%
3	**Failed**	45%	0%	10%	85%

A few   All   A lot   Most   None   Some

1. ___Some___ students in the class passed chemistry. _____ them failed chemistry.
2. _____ the students passed English. _____ the students failed it.
3. _____ the students passed geography. _____ students failed it.
4. _____ students passed geometry. _____ them failed it.

3 About you

Grammar and vocabulary Answer the questions with your own information. If you are still in high school, write about last year.

When you were in high school, what was a subject . . .

1. most of your friends liked? _Most of my friends liked P.E._____
2. all of the students had to study? _____
3. a lot of students hated? _____
4. some of your classmates loved? _____
5. no students ever failed? _____
6. a few students were always really good at? _____
7. none of your classmates liked? _____
8. a lot of students got good grades in? _____
9. some students dropped? _____

Correcting things you say

Conversation
strategies **Complete the conversations with the sentences in the box.**

> Actually, no, it was 2009.   Actually, I guess I spent some weekends with my grandparents.
> Well, at least most of them didn't.   Well, actually, we had a few problems. My dad lost his job.
> No, wait. I was nine.   ✓Well, not all of them. Josie speaks three languages.
> Well, actually, it was dark brown.   No, wait. . . . Her name was Mrs. Santos.
> Actually, no, I was 18 when I quit.

1. A All my friends are bilingual. They all speak two languages.
       Well, not all of them. Josie speaks three languages.

    B That's amazing!

2. A My best friend and I had sleepovers every weekend when we were kids.
       _____

    B That sounds like fun.

3. A We moved to Rio de Janeiro when I was ten.
       _____

    B So you were pretty young.

4. A I was on a swimming team until I was 16.
       _____

    B That's the reason you swim so well.

5. A My brother and I had a perfect childhood.
       _____

    B Really? But you were generally pretty happy, right?

6. A My cousin lived with us for a year – in 2010, I think.
       _____

    B That was your cousin Alice, right?

7. A My favorite teacher in elementary school was Mrs. Santana.
       _____

    B Oh, yeah? My favorite teacher was Mr. Stiller.

8. A When I was little, none of my friends had pets.
       _____

    B But you had a dog, right?

9. A I had black hair when I was born.
       _____

    B Really? I was born with no hair at all!

2 I mean

Conversation strategies | **Complete the questions using *I mean* to correct the underlined words. Then answer the questions.**

1. When you were a child, what was the name of your first <u>professor</u>, *I mean, teacher* ?

   _____

2. Were you six or seven when you started <u>high school</u>, _____ ?

   _____

3. In elementary school, did you have lunch in the school <u>gym</u>, _____ ?

   _____

4. When you were young, what was your favorite <u>sport</u>, _____ ?
   Did you like checkers? _____

5. When you were young, did you play any <u>music</u>, _____ , like the piano?

   _____

3 About you

Conversation strategies | **Complete these sentences so they are true for you.**

1. I started school when I was three. Actually, no,
   when I was five .

2. The name of my elementary school was Park Elementary.
   No, wait. . . . _____ .

3. My first teacher's name was Miss Parker, I mean,

   _____ .

4. I got good grades in every subject. Well, _____

   _____ .

5. Most of my childhood friends liked classical music. Well,
   no, _____ .

6. When I was a child, my favorite holiday was Halloween, I
   mean, _____ .

7. I remember all my classmates in kindergarten. Well, actually, _____ .

8. A lot of my friends did gymnastics or played sports after school.
   No, wait. . . . _____ .

9. We always had pizza for school lunch.
   Well, actually, _____ .

1 Small-town story

Reading **A** Read the story of Yolanda's life. Then number the pictures in the correct order.

Interview: A happy childhood by Kathy Montaño

Kathy Montaño grew up in the small town of Bagdad, Arizona. She interviewed several Mexican Americans in Bagdad about their childhood. This is the story of Yolanda Sandoval.

"My name is Yolanda Sandoval. I was born in Cananea, Mexico, on June 13, 1922. My parents brought me to Bagdad when I was six months old. My father's name was Francisco Sandoval, and my mother's name was Cecilia Bernal.

I was their first child. I have four younger brothers. My mother gave Rafael, my third brother, her name as a middle name. Apart from Rafael, no one had a middle name. My mother was very gentle and patient.

My father was very kind but strict. He worked in a mine. He didn't talk much about his work, maybe because he didn't like it. My mother didn't go out to work. She stayed home to take care of us.

My mother always did special things for our birthdays. One year she gave me a purple party. Everything was purple, even the drinks! She also made me a purple dress. That was the best party I ever had. I invited all my friends – except for Bobby. I was angry with him at the time. My mother died when I was 16. I still miss her.

My brothers and I loved the movies. We thought they were wonderful. A man named Angel Ruiz showed old cowboy movies at the local theater, and we went to all of them. He charged five cents for a movie. Sometimes we didn't have the five cents, but he let us see the movie anyway.

I loved school. I had to study English for four years, science for two (I took chemistry and biology), and a foreign language for two years. I took Spanish, of course! Spanish was easy for me, so I got good grades. I also studied U.S. history, home economics, and physical education. I was a good student."

B Read Yolanda's story again. Then complete the sentences.

1. Kathy Montaño interviewed several people in her town about *their childhood* .
2. Yolanda Sandoval came to Bagdad when she _____ .
3. Yolanda's father didn't talk much about his work because _____ .
4. On Yolanda's birthday one year, her mother gave her _____ .
5. At the local movie theater, Yolanda and her brothers saw _____ .
6. Yolanda studied English for _____ .

2 When I was a teenager

A Answer these questions about your first year in high school. If you are still in high school, talk about last year. Use *except (for)* or *apart from*.

1. Did you like your teachers?

   I liked all my teachers except for my history teacher, Mr. Crown.

2. Did you enjoy all your subjects?

   _____

3. Did you get along with all your classmates?

   _____

4. Did you and your best friend do a lot of things together?

   _____

B Write about some of your favorite activities when you were a teenager.

> When I was a teenager, I lived in
> My friends and I loved to

Unit 5 Progress chart

What can you do? Mark the boxes. ✓ = I can . . . ? = I need to review how to . . .	To review, go back to these pages in the Student's Book.
Grammar	
☐ make statements and ask questions with the simple past and past of *be*.	44 and 45
☐ talk about the past using time expressions.	44 and 45
☐ use determiners: *all (of), most (of), a lot of, some (of), a few (of), no, none of.*	46 and 47
Vocabulary	
☐ say years.	45
☐ name at least 12 school subjects.	47
☐ name at least 5 general subject categories.	47
Conversation strategies	
☐ correct things I say with expressions like *Actually* and *No, wait*.	48 and 49
☐ use *I mean* to correct myself.	49
Writing	
☐ use *except (for)* and *apart from* to link ideas.	51

Lesson A Finding places

 Where is it?

Grammar
and
vocabulary

Look at the map. Write two answers for each question.

FIRST AVENUE

Buy Right Electronics

ATMs

The Sports Shop

First National Bank

The Shoe Place

ELM STREET

Elm Cinema 6

Tesso Gas

The Bookmark Bookstore

parking

People's Drugstore

Flora's Flower Shop

Dan's Deli

Flowers for Less

Pearl Jewelry Store

SECOND AVENUE

Food Treasures Supermarket

Bloomington's Department Store

PINE STREET

Mickey's Sports Café

Fancy's Convenience Store

OAK STREET

Public Restrooms

THIRD AVENUE

1. Where's the bookstore?

It's on Pine Street, between the bank and the drugstore.
It's across the street from the gas station.

2. Where are the public restrooms?

3. Where's the parking lot?

4. Where are the ATMs?

5. Where's the gas station?

6. Where's the drugstore?

2 Looking for places

Grammar | **Write questions. Then complete the answers with *there's one*, *there are some*, *there isn't one*, or *there aren't any*.**

1. A _Is there a drugstore around here?_ _____
   (drugstore around here ?)

   B Yes, _there's one_ _____ on the corner of Pine Street and Second Avenue.

2. A _____
   (parking lot near here ?)

   B _____ on Oak Street, behind the bookstore.

3. A _____
   (ATMs anywhere ?)

   B _____ over there, across from the gas station.

4. A _____
   (museum in this town ?)

   B No, sorry, _____ .

5. A _____
   (outdoor cafés near here ?)

   B No, _____ outdoor cafés near here, but there are some restaurants
   inside the department store on Pine Street.

6. A _____
   (public restrooms around here ?)

   B Yeah, sure, _____ on Third Avenue.

3 About you

Grammar and vocabulary | **Write questions. Then answer the questions about your neighborhood.**

1. A (a good coffee shop) _Is there a good coffee shop in this neighborhood?_ _____
   B _Yes, there is. There's Emily's on the corner of Center Avenue and First Street._

2. A (a big department store) _____
   B _____

3. A (any unusual stores) _____
   B _____

4. A (a convenience store) _____
   B _____

5. A (any cheap restaurants) _____
   B _____

6. A (any ATMs) _____
   B _____

1 Places in town

Vocabulary | Complete the sentences with the places in the box.

aquarium	museum	running path	stadium	Visitor's Center
✓hotel	parking garage	skateboard ramp	theater	water park

You can . . .

1. sleep at a _____hotel_____ .
2. see sea animals at an _____ .
3. go jogging on a _____ .
4. go skateboarding on a _____ .
5. see a play at a _____ .
6. see art and interesting exhibits at a _____ .
7. ask for information at a _____ .
8. leave your car at a _____ .
9. watch a baseball game at a _____ .
10. swim in an outdoor pool at a _____ .

2 Where am I going?

Vocabulary | Some people are at the Sea View Hotel. Where do they want to go? Look at the map.
Complete the conversations with the names of the places.

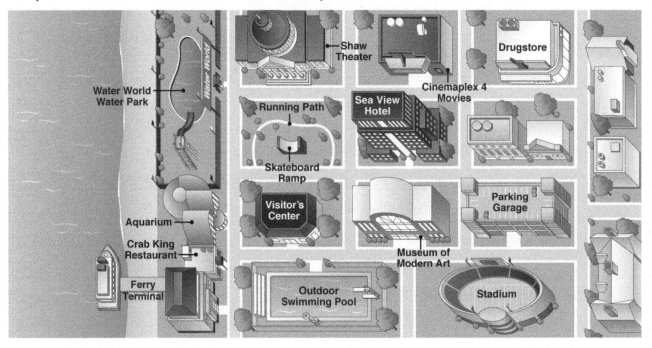

1. A Can you tell me how to get to the _____ ?

    B Sure. When you leave the hotel, turn right. It's on the next block. It's there on your right.

2. A Can you tell me how to get to the _____ ?

    B Yes. Go out of the hotel and turn left. Turn left again at the corner, go one block, and turn right.
    It's on your left.

3. A Can you help me? I'd like to go to the _____ .

    B Yes. Turn right out of the hotel. Go straight for another block and make a left.
    Walk two blocks. It's on your right, next to the restaurant.

3 Directions, directions

Grammar and vocabulary

Rewrite the sentences to make requests. Then look at the map on page 44 and write directions.

1. You're at the Visitor's Center. "Tell me how to get to the theater." (Could)

    A *Could you tell me how to get to the theater?*

    B *Sure. Turn right. Then take the first right. Walk straight ahead for two blocks.*
    The theater is going to be there across the street on your right.

2. You're at the aquarium. "Give me directions to the hotel." (Could)

    A _____

    B _____

3. You're at the aquarium. "Tell me how to get to the drugstore." (Can)

    A _____

    B _____

4. You're at the pool. "How do I get to the stadium?" (Can)

    A _____

    B _____

5. You're at the skateboard ramp. "Give me directions to the ferry terminal." (Could)

    A _____

    B _____

6. You're at the theater. "Tell me how to get to the parking garage." (Can)

    A _____

    B _____

4 About you

Grammar and vocabulary

Complete the offers and requests using *Can* or *Could*. Then answer the questions with true information about the neighborhood you are in now.

1. A _____ recommend a nice restaurant around here?

    B _____

2. A Excuse me. I need some help. _____ help me?

    B Sure. How _____ ?

    A _____ get to the nearest hotel?

    B _____

3. A _____ directions to a park or a place to go running?

    B _____

1 Checking information

Complete the conversations. Check the information.

1. A Hi. Where to?

   B I'm going to 830 Center Street.

   A *I'm sorry? Did you say*
      813 Center Street?

   B No, 830. That's on the corner of Center and
      Main – on the left side of the street.

   A _____
      _____

   B Yes, the left side.

2. A Could you tell me how to get to Atlantic
      Bank?

   B _____

   A Yes. Do you know it?

   B I think so. Go straight ahead for three
      blocks and turn left. It's on the right.

   A _____

   B No. Not on the left. It's on the right.

3. A Can I help you?

   B Yes, please. What time does the next show
      start?

   A At 7:15.

   B _____

   A 7:15.

   B And what time does it end?

   A It ends at 9:05.

   B _____

   A Yes, that's right.

4. A Can you give me directions to a pet store?

   B _____

   A No, not a bookstore – a pet store. I want to
      buy some new fish for my aquarium.

   B Oh. Let me think. I think there's a pet store
      at Bay Street Mall.

   A _____

   B Bay Street Mall. It's about half an hour from
      here.

2 I'm sorry?

Conversation
strategies
Complete the "echo" questions with the words in the box. Use each one only once.
There are two extra.

| how much | what | what kind | what time | when | where |

1. A A new deli opened right across the street from us.

    B I'm sorry, a new _____ opened?

    A A new deli. Let's try it. Then you don't need to cook!

2. A My brother spent almost five hundred dollars on theater
       tickets for his family.

    B Sorry? He spent _____ ?

    A Almost five hundred dollars. I hope it's a good show!

3. A I really want to leave at 6:00.

    B Sorry? You want to leave at _____ ?

    A At 6:00. Oh, it's already ten after. We're late!

4. A Did you remember? We're going to the aquarium today.

    B I'm sorry? We're going _____ ?

    A To the aquarium. Did you forget?

3 Questions, questions

Conversation
strategies
Complete the conversations with "echo" questions.

1. A Do you have your wallet? The tickets are
       60 dollars each.

    B They cost _how much?_

    A Sixty dollars each. Hurry. The show starts in
       15 minutes. At 3:00.

    B At _____ ?

    A At three. Hurry! It's going to be fun. There are going
       to be acrobats and things.

    B There are going to be _____ ?
       Um, maybe we should just go to a movie instead!

2. A Let's go to the park today. There's a new bike path.

    B A new _____ ?

    A A bike path. We can go cycling. And then we can go to Primm's.

    B We can go _____ ?

    A Primm's. It's an ice cream place near the park. It sells really good pistachio ice cream.

    B Um, OK. But wait, it sells _____ of ice cream?

1 Life down under

Reading **A Read the article about Coober Pedy. Check (✓) the items the article talks about.**

☐ an amusement park
☐ an underground hotel
☐ a rock and roll museum
☐ a place that looks like the moon
☐ a drive-in movie theater
☐ an opal mine

Coober Pedy ▫ ◻ ✕

COOBER PEDY
—THE OPAL CAPITAL OF THE WORLD

Welcome to the desert town of Coober Pedy in the outback of Australia. The name Coober Pedy comes from the Aboriginal words *kupa piti*, which mean "white man in a hole." We hope you'll come visit.

Explorers first found opals in this area on February 1, 1915. In 1946, an Aboriginal woman named Tottie Bryant dug out a large and valuable opal. After that, a lot of people came to Coober Pedy to mine opals.

During the 1960s, many European immigrants came to work here, and Coober Pedy quickly became a large modern town. Today, Coober Pedy is the world's main source of high-quality opals and a unique tourist spot.

It's so hot in Coober Pedy that a lot of people live underground! There are many underground homes, as well as underground hotels, museums, opal shops, art galleries, and, of course, opal mines.

Here are some places to visit during your stay.

Umoona Opal Mine & Museum is a unique underground museum about the history of the town. It includes a model underground home and a small opal mine. Some of the world's finest opals are on display here.

The Moon Plain is a large rocky area unlike anywhere else. It looks like the moon – or another planet! It was the

set for many movies, including *Mad Max Beyond Thunderdome, The Adventures of Priscilla, Queen of the Desert,* and *The Red Planet*. It is about 15 kilometers northeast of Coober Pedy.

Coober Pedy Drive-In is an open-air movie theater. You can see a movie there every other Saturday night.

B Read the article again. Then match the two parts of each sentence.

1. The name Coober Pedy means __d__
2. Tottie Bryant found _____
3. Coober Pedy became a modern mining town when _____
4. Right now, Coober Pedy is the world's main source _____
5. As a tourist place, Coober Pedy is famous for _____
6. The Moon Plain was _____

a. the set for many movies.
b. a very big and valuable opal.
c. its underground homes, museums, stores, and mines.
✓d. "white man in a hole."
e. immigrants came to work in the mines.
f. of high-quality opals.

2 Walking guide

Writing **A Read this New Orleans walking tour. Look at the map and fill in the missing words.**

❶ This is the Garden District Book Shop. Anne Rice, a famous author from New Orleans, calls this her favorite bookstore.

❷ Take Prytania Street ___*four*___ blocks to Philip Street. Turn _____ on Philip Street. Take Philip Street one _____ to Coliseum Street. _____ a right on Coliseum Street. The homes on the _____ are called the Seven Sisters. A man wanted his seven daughters to live close to him. He built these seven houses for them as wedding gifts.

❸ Go _____ on Coliseum Street and walk to the end of the block. _____ left on First Street. Go _____ for one block. It's right there, on the _____ . This is the Brevard-Mahat-Rice House, where Anne Rice lives and works.

B Think of two tourist attractions in your town or city. Write directions from one to the other.

> *Start at*

Unit 6 Progress chart

What can you do? Mark the boxes. ✓ = I can . . . ? = I need to review how to . . .	To review, go back to these pages in the Student's Book.
Grammar	
☐ use *Is there?* and *Are there?* to ask about places in a town.	54 and 55
☐ use *across from*, *behind*, *between*, etc., to describe location.	55
☐ make offers and requests with *Can* and *Could*.	56 and 57
Vocabulary	
☐ name at least 15 places in a city or town.	54, 55, and 56
Conversation strategies	
☐ check information by repeating key words and using "checking" expressions.	58 and 59
☐ ask "echo" questions to check information.	59
Writing	
☐ write a guide giving directions.	61

Illustration credits

Ken Batelman: 42, 44   **Lisa Blackshear:** 24   **Domninic Bugatto:** 14, 34, 82, 83   **Cambridge University Press:** 25, 27, 49, 52
Daniel Chen: 6, 94   **Matt Collins:** 40   **Chuck Gonzales:** 19, 29, 67, 75, 85, 96   **Frank Montagna:** 10, 22, 30, 58, 59, 69, 78
Marilena Perilli: 5, 66, 70, 85   **Greg White:** 20, 47, 62, 63, 91   **Terry Wong:** 2, 3, 28, 55, 61

Photo credits

4 *(clockwise from top left)* ©JupiterImages; ©Monkey Business Images/Shutterstock; ©Alan Thornton/Getty Images; ©YURI KADOBNOV/AFP/Getty Images; ©Ocean/Corbis; ©Punchstock   **8** ©Kjpargeter/Shutterstock   **11** ©Image Source/SuperStock   **12** *(top row, left to right)* ©Henry Diltz/Corbis; ©Charles Sykes/Associated Press; ©Matt Kent/WireImage/Getty Images; ©Frank Micelotta/Getty Images *(top row, left to right)* ©Barros & Barros/Getty Images; ©Tim Mosenfelder/Corbis; ©Al Bello/Getty Images; ©Peter Kramer/NBC/NBCU Photo Bank via Getty Images   **13** *(top to bottom)* ©Jason Merritt/Getty Images For BET; ©Jon Kopaloff/FilmMagic/Getty Images
15 *(left to right)* ©Thinkstock; ©Sebastien Starr/Getty Images   **16** *(background)* ©tdixon8875/Shutterstock   **18** *(top to bottom)* ©Image Source/Getty Images; ©Digital Vision/Getty Images   **21** *(clockwise from top left)* ©Mary Kate Denny/PhotoEdit; ©Dana White/PhotoEdit; ©Thinkstock; ©Jose Luis Pelaez Inc./Corbis   **25** ©Punchstock   **26** *(top to bottom)* ©Gregg DeGuire/WireImage/Getty Images; ©Russ Einhorn 2004/Russ Einhorn/Splash News/Newscom; ©Jason LaVeris/FilmMagic/Getty Images; ©Gregg DeGuire/WireImage/Getty Images; ©Jason LaVeris/FilmMagic/Getty Images; ©Alex Livesey - FIFA/FIFA via Getty Images   **31** ©Keren Su/China Span/Alamy
32 *(top to bottom)* ©Anna-Mari West/Shutterstock; ©Africa Studio/Shutterstock   **35** ©Michael Newman/PhotoEdit   **39** ©Michael Newman/PhotoEdit   **46** *(left to right)* ©Blend Images/SuperStock; ©Andersen Ross/Getty Images   **48** *(top to bottom)* ©Joel Arem/Getty Images; ©HUGHES Herve/hemis.fr/Getty Images; ©Andrew Watson/Getty Images   **50** ©Ralph Lee Hopkins/Getty Images
51 ©Dave Fleetham/Pacific Stock - Design Pics/SuperStock *(background)* ©sdecoret/Shutterstock   **53** *(left to right)* ©Thinkstock; ©Jupiterimages/Thinkstock   **54** *(top to bottom)* ©Greg Elms/Getty Images; ©Michael Goldman/Masterfile   **56** *(left to right)* ©Purcell Team/Alamy; ©DIOMEDIA/Alamy; ©Peter Grant/Getty Images   **57** ©Trish Punch/Getty Images   **64** Photos Courtesy of Poezenboot
68 *(top to bottom)* ©Thinkstock; ©Punchstock   **76** *(left to right)* ©PhotoInc/Getty Images; ©Kablonk/SuperStock   **77** ©Dougal Waters/Getty Images   **80** ©Raoul Minsart/Masterfile *(background)* ©Kjpargeter/Shutterstock   **82** ©David Lees/Getty Images
84 *(top to bottom)* ©Punchstock; ©largeformat4x5/Getty Images; ©Seth Resnick/Science Faction/SuperStock   **86** *(top to bottom)* ©Maximiliano Failla/AFP/Getty Images; ©Shaun Botterill - FIFA/FIFA via Getty Images; ©STR/AFP/Getty Images; ©s_bukley/Shutterstock   **87** *(top to bottom)* ©David Cannon/Getty Images; ©Ric Francis/Associated Press; ©DFree/Shutterstock; ©cinemafestival/Shutterstock; ©Clive Brunskill/Getty Images; ©Elnur/Shutterstock; ©Amos Morgan/Thinkstock; ©Thinkstock; ©Jupiterimages/Thinkstock   **88** *(left to right)* ©imagebroker.net/SuperStock; ©Iain McKell/Getty Images; ©Masterfile; ©Nick Dolding/Getty Images; ©Ellen Stagg/Getty Images; ©Thinkstock *(background)* ©alex.makarova/Shutterstock   **92** *(left column, top to bottom)* ©Punchstock; ©George Doyle/Thinkstock; ©George Doyle & Ciaran Griffin/Thinkstock; ©Jack Hollingsworth/Getty Images; ©Corbis; ©Thinkstock *(middle column, top to bottom)* ©Jupiterimages/Thinkstock; ©Thinkstock; ©Jeff Greenberg/PhotoEdit; ©David Young-Wolff/PhotoEdit; ©Michael Newman/PhotoEdit; ©Tetra Images/Getty Images *(right column, top to bottom)* ©Tom Carter/PhotoEdit; ©Jupiterimages/Thinkstock; ©Thinkstock; ©Flying Colours Ltd/Getty Images; ©Robin Nelson/PhotoEdit; ©JupiterImages

Text credits

While every effort has been made, it has not always been possible to identify the sources of all the material used, or to trace all copyright holders. If any omissions are brought to our notice, we will be happy to include the appropriate acknowledgements on reprinting.

The top 500 spoken words

This is a list of the top 500 words in spoken North American English. It is based on a sample of four and a half million words of conversation from the Cambridge International Corpus. The most frequent word, *I*, is at the top of the list.

1. I	40. really	79. see
2. and	41. with	80. how
3. the	42. he	81. they're
4. you	43. one	82. kind
5. uh	44. are	83. here
6. to	45. this	84. from
7. a	46. there	85. did
8. that	47. I'm	86. something
9. it	48. all	87. too
10. of	49. if	88. more
11. yeah	50. no	89. very
12. know	51. get	90. want
13. in	52. about	91. little
14. like	53. at	92. been
15. they	54. out	93. things
16. have	55. had	94. an
17. so	56. then	95. you're
18. was	57. because	96. said
19. but	58. go	97. there's
20. is	59. up	98. I've
21. it's	60. she	99. much
22. we	61. when	100. where
23. huh	62. them	101. two
24. just	63. can	102. thing
25. oh	64. would	103. her
26. do	65. as	104. didn't
27. don't	66. me	105. other
28. that's	67. mean	106. say
29. well	68. some	107. back
30. for	69. good	108. could
31. what	70. got	109. their
32. on	71. OK	110. our
33. think	72. people	111. guess
34. right	73. now	112. yes
35. not	74. going	113. way
36. um	75. were	114. has
37. or	76. lot	115. down
38. my	77. your	116. we're
39. be	78. time	117. any

The top 500 spoken words

118. he's	161. five	204. sort
119. work	162. always	205. great
120. take	163. school	206. bad
121. even	164. look	207. we've
122. those	165. still	208. another
123. over	166. around	209. car
124. probably	167. anything	210. true
125. him	168. kids	211. whole
126. who	169. first	212. whatever
127. put	170. does	213. twenty
128. years	171. need	214. after
129. sure	172. us	215. ever
130. can't	173. should	216. find
131. pretty	174. talking	217. care
132. gonna	175. last	218. better
133. stuff	176. thought	219. hard
134. come	177. doesn't	220. haven't
135. these	178. different	221. trying
136. by	179. money	222. give
137. into	180. long	223. I'd
138. went	181. used	224. problem
139. make	182. getting	225. else
140. than	183. same	226. remember
141. year	184. four	227. might
142. three	185. every	228. again
143. which	186. new	229. pay
144. home	187. everything	230. try
145. will	188. many	231. place
146. nice	189. before	232. part
147. never	190. though	233. let
148. only	191. most	234. keep
149. his	192. tell	235. children
150. doing	193. being	236. anyway
151. cause	194. bit	237. came
152. off	195. house	238. six
153. I'll	196. also	239. family
154. maybe	197. use	240. wasn't
155. real	198. through	241. talk
156. why	199. feel	242. made
157. big	200. course	243. hundred
158. actually	201. what's	244. night
159. she's	202. old	245. call
160. day	203. done	246. saying

The top 500 spoken words

247. dollars	290. started	333. believe
248. live	291. job	334. thinking
249. away	292. says	335. funny
250. either	293. play	336. state
251. read	294. usually	337. until
252. having	295. wow	338. husband
253. far	296. exactly	339. idea
254. watch	297. took	340. name
255. week	298. few	341. seven
256. mhm	299. child	342. together
257. quite	300. thirty	343. each
258. enough	301. buy	344. hear
259. next	302. person	345. help
260. couple	303. working	346. nothing
261. own	304. half	347. parents
262. wouldn't	305. looking	348. room
263. ten	306. someone	349. today
264. interesting	307. coming	350. makes
265. am	308. eight	351. stay
266. sometimes	309. love	352. mom
267. bye	310. everybody	353. sounds
268. seems	311. able	354. change
269. heard	312. we'll	355. understand
270. goes	313. life	356. such
271. called	314. may	357. gone
272. point	315. both	358. system
273. ago	316. type	359. comes
274. while	317. end	360. thank
275. fact	318. least	361. show
276. once	319. told	362. thousand
277. seen	320. saw	363. left
278. wanted	321. college	364. friends
279. isn't	322. ones	365. class
280. start	323. almost	366. already
281. high	324. since	367. eat
282. somebody	325. days	368. small
283. let's	326. couldn't	369. boy
284. times	327. gets	370. paper
285. guy	328. guys	371. world
286. area	329. god	372. best
287. fun	330. country	373. water
288. they've	331. wait	374. myself
289. you've	332. yet	375. run

The top 500 spoken words

376. they'll	418. company	460. sorry
377. won't	419. friend	461. living
378. movie	420. set	462. drive
379. cool	421. minutes	463. outside
380. news	422. morning	464. bring
381. number	423. between	465. easy
382. man	424. music	466. stop
383. basically	425. close	467. percent
384. nine	426. leave	468. hand
385. enjoy	427. wife	469. gosh
386. bought	428. knew	470. top
387. whether	429. pick	471. cut
388. especially	430. important	472. computer
389. taking	431. ask	473. tried
390. sit	432. hour	474. gotten
391. book	433. deal	475. mind
392. fifty	434. mine	476. business
393. months	435. reason	477. anybody
394. women	436. credit	478. takes
395. month	437. dog	479. aren't
396. found	438. group	480. question
397. side	439. turn	481. rather
398. food	440. making	482. twelve
399. looks	441. American	483. phone
400. summer	442. weeks	484. program
401. hmm	443. certain	485. without
402. fine	444. less	486. moved
403. hey	445. must	487. gave
404. student	446. dad	488. yep
405. agree	447. during	489. case
406. mother	448. lived	490. looked
407. problems	449. forty	491. certainly
408. city	450. air	492. talked
409. second	451. government	493. beautiful
410. definitely	452. eighty	494. card
411. spend	453. wonderful	495. walk
412. happened	454. seem	496. married
413. hours	455. wrong	497. anymore
414. war	456. young	498. you'll
415. matter	457. places	499. middle
416. supposed	458. girl	500. tax
417. worked	459. happen	